ARE NOT
OUR LOWING HEIFERS
SLEEKER THAN
NIGHT-SWOLLEN
MUSHROOMS?

Nada Gordon

SPUYTENDUYVIL

ISBN 1-881471-66-7
TITLE BY JOHN KEATS
DRAWINGS BY GARY SULLIVAN

A C K N O W L E D G M E N T S

SOME OF THESE POEMS HAVE APPEARED IN THE FOLLOWING JOURNALS:
Cello Entry, ReadMe, Lungfull!, AND How2. "VALUE = AGE X
RAGE" WAS NO. 70(E) IN THE Oasia broadside series. THANKS TO ALL
THE EDITORS.

I WROTE THESE POEMS IN 1999-2000 IN NEW YORK (OFTEN ON THE F
TRAIN BETWEEN BROOKLYN AND MANHATTAN). THEY WOULD NOT HAVE
COME INTO BEING HAD GARY SULLIVAN NOT LURED ME OVER THE
OCEAN FROM TOKYO. TO HIM, BOUNDLESS GRATITUDE AND LOVE.

THANKS ALSO TO YOU, DEAR READER, FOR YOUR ATTENTION: yoroshiku
onegai itashimasu.

SPUYTENDUYVIL DOT NET
1-800-886-5304

for Gary, Dante, & Nemo

The things I notice when
I want to write are
Not the things I think about
or feel they are what
Gets sucked through the
Hole I punch in time

—Jordan Davis
"When I was the Subject"

CONTENTS

LADY LANGUISH.

16 Why are comic songs like gross
blunders?

HER PRE-HARP SHAPE I

The quality   of a painter's ear,
then,
        tones,

depends on the, um,

                being

        in his* landscape.

Pursuing   the perfect
        cream:

                Any operatic deed's one normal

The truth is
        that old folktale

For the lonely violin is,
tan or chest,
Rome

                Doth, as a credo, rat?

*her

Oh riotous!

I can gel,
I can dairy whether
'tis chorale
or chamber piece

I can,
while listening to ammunition,
ice sweater

They vowed eternal love and somehow

the movie with the most chilling fever: "I"
—shadowy choice—

ran
down
my

spine.

CLOVA MOWDIS

> I became a fabulous opera.
> —Arthur Rimbaud

WHEN THE VOICE IS
IRRESISTIBLY ATTRACTED
TO THE PITCH OF THE
NEXT TONE, YOU CAN
SING. haaaa.* the joey
survives on the midriff,
the poem on sugar, the song
on wireless pivot. just
"droned" or "got through"
is illegal. INSTEAD, YOUR
CONSCIOUS ACT MUST RESULT
FROM YOUR INSTINCTIVE
"URGE." shift. drusilla loves
the larynxes, up in trees,
prowling. i am really grow-
ling as a poet. darla loves
the thorniness in the gentle
sesame arm. i love the gold
maple leaf hidden in the
immigrant corset, the
caraway tongue, though
today's head's talk's just
irritant groove genre.

*arpeggio

the rhythm i wanted
to hear was further,
longer, happier than
you can think. "DESTROY
THE INTELLECT BY MEANS
OF THE INTELLECT." i was
just thinking: "THINK
OF ME ONLY WITH YOUR
MIND, AND I WILL THINK
WITH MINE." the giant
lure floats before, psych-
edelic, with tourmaline
plumes. my panties are
sticky with nuttiness.
screeeeeeeeeeeeeeeeech.
TO BRING WORD AND TONE
TO THE LIPS WITHOUT LOSING
DARKER RESONANCE IS
AN ABSOLUTE NECESSITY, as if
"allergic to salt" or "it's
hissssing." there's something
kicky on my ankles: jade spice
scallop (fidgeting). hey bozo,
c'mere and kiss my quivering . . .
ellipses . . . the room is . . .
quivering, as aspic (no
peppercorns). YOUR VOICE

WILL CONTINUE FOCUSED IN YOUR
SKULL SO LONG AS YOU SING WITH
REGULAR VIBRATION IN THE THROAT,
FED BY COMPRESSED BREATH,
CONTROLLED BY THE PELVIS. if
you do your good work,
there will be a golden pea.
the art you practice may
be your own, coiled at
clavicle as "abbess" or
"lightning"—frenetic
gypsy vibraphone in
subway we stop to
gape our ears at. in
the tinder box, dogs
with "saucer eyes." there
is so much to write about
queen elizabeth, bamboo,
seahorse, a tiger and the
kanji for tiger. how like a
jumpy flea or pixie the
grasped-for "essence" of
the writing. it's time,
i guess, squeezed up as
dough through fist but palm
is almost empty smelling
of yeast. HEARING IN ADVANCE

YOURSELF SINGING THE TONE
IS THE CAUSE OF THIS WEIRD
SENSATION. dante gnaws
the corner of the notebook,
touches pink nose moist
to my toe. they are pouncing.
were. feel whiskers on foot,
little velvet body does a white-
bellied, ringtailed stretch. "i
have no spirit for codcake."
"we're out of codcake," but
the writing serves as codicil
to me, my little body a mean
bull elephant, conservative,
on codeine, i glower to hear
she wears glitter. awk,
levity, the almond swing
of curiousity. T=A=N=T=
R=U=M. as erect penis is
hector but me virgin and
jules who said no and no and
no. can you imagine a big
prehistoric belly all hanging
over your back and whispering
"je t'aime!" "je t'aime!" there
really is no cul-de-sac that writing

can not charge through, a kind of
didactic negligée. WORDS ARE
BUT DYES THAT TINT THE FOCUSED
VIBRATION OF THE VOICE WITH THEIR
COLORS. "we'd like to shoot a film,
would you like to be the star?"
OBJECTIVITY ALONE IS UNRESTFUL,
AWKWARD, AND RIGID. OBJECTIVITY
ALONE PRODUCES ORGANIZED
STUPIDITY, i.e. "slim crescent
moons about in the sky," a
tangle of raincoats, umbrellas
in a muse. flat white shells
fall in clinking heaps. handsome
actor says, "here, duckweed,"
and i look and there's something
genuine. i never spill a drop but
thinking makes it cruel
world and its internal slamming,
violence. irregular twitching
and curio. did the cats eat?
my tongue twists in my mouth.
image? or glitter? lungs?
or gills? erotics take the place
of thinking. i lie down on
the floor in contempt of
the gummy price sticker

on the still-life. price tags
on everything, and the heat
in ruffled sleeves on bandstand.
sleeping an ordeal. i slept as
CLENCH, no hand on pubis:
emballage. we are good
conduits. i would write
anything now as sentry
or savior, button king carving.
"what are you, paul bunyan?"
the relaxation of sophistry:
choking victim. please just
messenger it to me, in gold
headband. QUIET THROAT.
SINGING IS INSTINCTIVE. ITS
CONTROL SUBCONSCIOUS, EACH
VOICE A LAW UNTO ITSELF. "BREATHE
THROUGH YOUR TONE." "if you are
magnetic, the world is yours."
ALL TONES (words) ARE "CLOSED"
UNTIL "OPENED" (grasped at).
THEY BREATHE OR EMANATE AS
sputterings (stigmata), gaspings
(peppercorns), hiccoughings,
gruntings (hypothalmus), wheezings
(frenzy), tremblings, scoopings,

slidings, sobbings, (culture),
cracklings, raspings (meanderings
of quail through underbrush),
bellowings, etc. THE FIXED
HIGH CHEST A VENTRILOQUAL EFFECT
called "long road" or "sensuous
thrill"—marlo thomas as caviar
with antinomies. orange
canary wing, where do you get
your vocabulary, your flip-haired
girls in the act of . . . dishevelment . . .
fuck . . . careful . . . if you want
nookie . . . or noise as naked
skeleton in sequins. NEVER
SEPARATE DICTION FROM SINGING,
NOT EVEN IN THOUGHT. my breasts
closer to soul than bladder, i have
trouble seeing past the light
of the gazelles. the trash
compactor within expands
to crunch sequins and steller's
jays, as if all i could think of
were the marbles in her mouth.
sister justice closet is it criminal
enough. slow down dragon of
i can't no, please change the sounds.

MENTALLY, THERE IS NO SILENCE,
YOU ARE EITHER SINGING A TONE OR
SPINNING THE INTERVAL BETWEEN
THAT AND THE NEXT PITCH. "my
writing has energy," i gloat,
"i'm working on an awesome
long poem," like that makes me
a debutante. with friends.
THIS IS THE LAW OF CONTINUITY
OF VIBRATION AND ENERGY. of
what do we speak when we
say "energy" in "writing"?
is it fascinating like a little
forbidden pharmaceutical
replacement drip? pure
innocent knowledge? egg-
drop? ok it is all tired and
sloppy and fascinating as if
this were the lower east side of
notebooks, or the glossy picture
of queen esther in veils. red lantern
shredding off its encirclements,
the hoop skirts that welcome
oblivion. "i didn't mean to be
so prickly. i'm sorry." but
the lantern is tattered, not

prickly. the bicycle sways
diagonally on its axis, we're
on the third planet from the
nuclear snooze button the
clapboard vicar pushes and
the crowd howls. and they do
howl. the tears spill out
like jujubees but clearer,
warmer. it's a subtle
activism, as if my lewd
gestures weren't enough—
well, they aren't, and i can't
go overboard 'cuz i'm not
totally on board. ANOTHER
ILLUSION IS "MY OTHER SELF"
(A SIXTH SENSE) THAT STANDS AT
A DISTANCE AND TELLS ME WHAT,
WHEN AND HOW TO DO . . . a kitten
stampede. the kittens stampede.
there are articles and there are
indefinite articles. carousel:
"GIRLS GIRLS GIRLS." there is only
a contrived . . . sluice gate. there
are patterns of longing (triangular)
that can be identified and boxed.

oh. my. the dictionary wants
my peeping snake's head's scumbag
tics. i want its ornery pink asters.
no synasthaesia. i would not have
come to this city alone as a blue
face coming out of an apple, even so
there's one of those ripcord
zzz-zzz-zzz helicopters, with
chives and not completely, hey
do you still love me? is there
any coconut? speech! speech!
CELL INTELLIGENCE (SENSATION AND
MUSCLE THROUGHOUT THE BODY)
AND ATOMIC POWER (REACTIONS
THAT PERVADE THE WHOLE BODY
AND PRODUCE COORDINATED ENERGY)
ARE THE TWO MAIN FACTORS IN
SINGING. she has a monkey of
learning (not of dots) on her
shirt. then: mustard. no go.
otherwise leopard orchard
affiliate. the goofy boots are on the
fish imprinted in the floor of the, um,
helicopter . . . that functions as a trope.
fighting and flighting trying to get out
of the horse into the helicopter. stupid

stable left margin the words bang
back to and catapult out to greet
each other with clasping, genitals
bulging or twingeing, in white
bodysuits, and this great music —
1960's synthesizer in cars that flip
over and make airplane sounds.
NOT UNTIL THE FOCUS OF THE VOICE
IS LIKE A FIXÉD STAR IN YOUR HEAD,
KEPT IN POSITION BY THE POWERS
INSIDE AND OUTSIDE YOUR BODY,
CAN YOU SING. not until the
tambourine makes contact with
the thigh in striped miniskirt
and the man at the piano in the
vest stops talking can the dancers
come out and make ontogeny
recapitulate phylogeny. their
vertebrae as amoeba, shrimp,
bird and monkey. their hands
crawl along their backs, one
elbow pointed at the sky,
the other at "newness." it's
how you feel in the orchestration
that gives the party of graceful

thought: "i don't think i
remember how to act." that's
what we mean when we speak
of "the personal," i.e. gary reads
o'hara to me in bed and suddenly
i want to write a poem with mike
and patsy in it. voilá! the next time
i look at my poem there indeed are
mike and patsy, and with sardines
(salty!). it's a kind of drug
program for individuals. "THE
INDIVIDUAL IS GOD." "THE INDI-
VIDUAL SPILLS (OVER?) INTO THE
INDIVIDUAL." "no one wants
to make transcendent art about
themselves (day)." no . . . one?
does it destruct in light?
are you free or not? IF PRONOUN-
CING WORDS "CLOSES" THE THROAT,
BLAME THE BREATH. LOOSE BREATH
WILL FURNISH NO RAYS OF VIBRATION,
HUMAN CONNECTION, jonquils, love,
LOSS, HATE, fawn lilies, envy,
STORY, SUBTERFUGE, natal plums,
dance, LIQUID, SOLID, gas (air?)
(aether?), BEARDED IRISES, PREDICTION,

flame violets, predictability,
SURPRISE, AWE, agapanthus,
romance, PINKS, SEXUALITY,
chiarascuro, inflection, COLUMBINES,
ACCENT, birds-of-paradise,
spice, DIRECTION, SAXIFRAGE,
connotation, freedom, AGREEMENT,
BUCKWHEAT, impatiens, duration,
OR THE CONSTANT BUOYANCY IN
HEAD, NECK AND UPPER CHEST
ESSENTIAL TO FREE TONE PRODUCTION
AND GOOD DICTION.

coda   (from ♪ Lamperti):

THE SINGING VOICE IS A "CASTLE IN THE AIR."

imagination is its architect.

NERVES CARRY OUT THE PLANS.

muscles are the laborers.

THE SOUL INHABITS IT.

coda ♭ to coda:

d e a r   other creature,
closing its eyes
in your head

in piquant

cathexis.

(sprinkled liberally with quotes from
Vocal Wisdom, the maxims of
Giovanni Battista Lamperti)

FANNY FANDANGO.

28 Why are butchers the strongest men in creation?

HER PRE-HARP SHAPE II

Reaper cuts edges off, revealing perception.

Pin edges down.

Regressive condition just halfway spelled out
internally is the height of Japanese painting.

Knowledge of a mystery song is disseminated.

With concealed cloaking, fool Jew.

I speak interminably,
I see with my ears:
I lean towards the center.

How does the bluebird cross the road?

Cutups celebrated end of strife in lower back.

It reverberates in stone bottles.

Muses can be downers.

FLESHSCAPE

To make a cape
of flesh, take
the labia minora
between the thumb
and forefinger, s-t-r-e-t-c-h
downwards and back
over the buttocks, then
upward along the ribcage,
curling them over
shoulders. Using palms,
rub the end flaps
onto the pectorals.
They will stick to the body
surface warmly, smelling
of minerals and cream,
their rosy hue ideal
for summer evenings.

To make a column
of flesh, pinch
the labia majora
between the eyelids,
s-t-r-e-t-c-h upwards
to the lilting sky
over rosy hillocks
and further
as an entertainment
for the pantheon.
Using balms, rub
the end flaps
onto the goddesses.
They will stick
to the body surface
warmly, in drapes
and folds, smelling
of conflict, their salmon
hue painting the firmament
they wave around in.

Lose the cares
of the flesh. Abstract
the fluid from the eyes.
Rub well into icons,
perfuming those milky
ludic globes. Spread
it as a carpet for
the lovelorn—their
digitalis. Conflict
is the balm of reason—
abstract, gratuitous,
baroque—as this.
Sunset comes with
multiple warnings,
filling the redolent
body with salmon.
And this labor.

The name of the beloved
may suddenly appear
as welts on that
forcibly externalized
internal skin, say "Mary"
or "Harry" or "Larry,"
a lighter whitish-red,
almost pussy; the discourse
suddenly twangs.
The candle steps out
from behind the eyes,
reveals itself to be
a candle. This is what I mean
by "self as destroyer."

"Could you just
scoot over a little
bit I don't have
enough room"

"I have a mean streak
of musicality."

To make a jailbreak
of flesh, clasp
the larva till it hardens
and tributaries crackle
up. If you are still
confined by the form,
consider the pleasure
of the otters. Your
phoenix will transmogrify
as other sorts of plumage
that may well singe
in sun, waves of heat
rising to begin
disintegration (a kind
of unfolding).

If you are still confused
by the form, invoke
its creator, its secret
prey. Jolly with
composition, she
has stretched
her lower lip up
over her head, and
the lyres (whipped
by a freak wind)'re all
abloom with
this (red light. dis-
tract) caco-
phany.

ARTICUA (ARAUCANA)

dressed as a coupla birdwings
angled to show flaws

pony   leans back
             on rice

     hesitating
speech   butterflies

Mabel and her inserts: the law
       of laughing at hazard.

the belle wants
to construct herself
    as vacuum

in antiquity.

what's happening?

1) number three
2) number nine

that's a great line   of celery

37

by the avant-garde marigolds

i hoem the hope in livery

past not negating
the meow of the nomad—

her juicy pups and minstrelsy

the quality of pondwater is not strained
nor are these verses' intimations.

i see water in the end.
it's fancy. (all kerfluffle)

farfalle
as edible gaiety: i eat
my
neck.

CHINCOTEAGUE

Out of the lark's tantalizéd face

sudden discotheque of

lies.

Juice, moss,
the clouds
seen as articles
of cold bewildering

The medium filled with brain.

Effete, girl-like snails,
on plasticene.

Arbitrary
pure faces
shrink.

I want to be
enveloped by beautiful
hymns. Harmonize.

A contraction lathered with
emotion.

spotted weeper.

rashes, carnation.
Rather than contiguity,
squares, circles.

I try to write it as a chant.
Now, an even vocable.

Limb to card, its liquid
sheet.

It paints movement.

Flung out.

Color and color, the
rational oddity's

fortunate skull
inside.

(after Kimberly Lyons)

Freedom of Woman

Here at our sea-washed, suntan gaudiness shall stand
A mighty wombat with a torpedo, whose flap
Is the imprisoned lignification, and her nape
Motif of Exodus. From her beamish hand-organ
Glows world-wide welter; her mild eyeholes command
The albino-brilliant hardihood that twin clairvoyants frame.
"Keep ancient languets, your storied pompoms," cries she
With silicone lisps. "Give me your tissues, your poppies,
Your humdrum matadors yearning to impregnate me.
The wretched regalia to your telegenic shiver.
Send these, the homologous, tenebrous, to me.
I lift my lanugo beside the golden dormouse."

(after Emma Lazarus)

2008

Am I the same one, that
spontaneous mucilage seeming
hollowed out from the loam but
pictorial or untrained element?

My dwarf the one of little faith living thing
grows increasingly aromatic of
civilization I'm too exquisite for it, tuneful
alloy of critique thus rent asunder

by intervals, can the Eighties be over?
by appendages and kosher studies of truth
Annihilation Seraphs over again?
Sovereign of line on the face seaweed he warbles

fastidiously lavish and fluent
Maybe epithelium cleaving monk near at hand
asymmetrical because of special varieties
of pedagogic hollow cube stylus white gold

they are growing old together into
archetypal generation which is a dwarf star
or effulgence, I am
frivolous or debilitated with cold feet so I

vocalize like a sweet but am unchaste like
a vibratory pose the ornaments
passing above a smooth as glass inky repose
to enchant sirocco and surf I

become a claw-shaped husk, one
without a synagogue
I ensnare the pacific I get moustache blossoms
and heartache generators which love me back for

the bubbling of it, kingdom come debris are the
decided spiritual beings on the wireless
a second's tatami waste a
cylinder drizzle then back into life sex.

She disentangles a framework of the senses
the law of smash the redoubled claw
closes into the motif S for the person in question or
robust chagrin or hovel or unshorn

the flesh flesh tolls the will will
signals the flesh will widens
with scrutiny the rhetorician addresses witnesses
and they are each other

idolatry of all moving pictures and optic receivers (eyes).

(after Alice Notley)

EXAGGERATION

The rings we see our dejections in
have no time to remake themselves as real rings.
Yet dejection is queen: of what? Not me
unless I roam the prairie, am sewn up
as a trope I can only see when ill.
I am never ill, but my red skin is.
I put on the ache-y catsuit
and feel the blinding mayhem. It's moot
to be so leaden in the head.
I must be a redhead. But even the living
eye and I refuse idle wishing
and so become . . . "shhh." It's benign.
Better to be a sick wish in thinking despond
than pose with poems and books.
The thought makes me a sleazy snatch.
As the book's sent from the poems' thinking
I notice the wish is too dizzy seeing the dejection
in what's left of the daughter to hook me with surprise.
Well, the night as hell shook me.
But after being polygraphed along lies of me
you claw my back. Afraid of what it'd do
inside of me?

(after Chris Stroffolino)

THE SECOND SECOND COMING

Writhing and moaning in the glistening fur,
The phallus cannot feel more vaginal;
Things stick upward, the pudendas tightly held;
Fierce orgasm's juice is on the girl.
The blood-cream tide is loosed, and everywhere
The ceremony of Priapus is found.
The breasts fondle all condoms, while the spurts
Are full of passionate mayonnaise.

Surely something Rabelaisian is at hand;
Surely the Second Coming is at hand.
The Second Coming! Hardly is the sperm out,
When a brassy image out of Clitoris Randy
Diddles my night. Somewhere in the hands of a hedonist,
A shape with a live body giving head to a man,
Aroused, naked, and guiltless as the sun,
Is moving her smooth thighs, while all about her
Reel shadows of provocative wild chicks.
The blanket drops again; but now I know
That twenty centuries of horny sleep
Were coaxed to emission by a rocking couple.
And what love beast, its bower hung round with ass
Touches the ludicrous on its horn?

(after W.B. Yeats)

LADY LOVEWELL.

12 Why are lover's sighs like long stockings?

HER PRE-HARP SHAPE III

or

Their Serpentine Union Complete,
The Male Snake Withdraws
His Crimson Penis

kissed on the ear, transported, spent
flip disputing facts involving the other vowels
first showed alarm during carousel . . .
throw around dance, laugh, illegally—it's shady
it has the average name
having no will to speak after put-down
with showy flower spray. threatening
boil has burst end, fruit raised to take in taste
of apricots—i have love for each one reared.
awkward—me too—as you feel it in your bones.
the top came off a fallen star, the higher power
not your only odds: baroque entablature
that can't be doctored. offbeat combos—
they're measured in eighths "The Outcome
of Mine Heart" (type this again). Time before
the day is ever detailed . . .

Undo Insertion:
Repeat Insertion

with showy flower spray. threatening
throw around dance, laugh, illegally—it's shady
it has the average name
they're measured in eighths "The Outcome
the top came off a fallen star, the higher power
the day is ever detailed!
that can't be doctored. offbeat combos—
of Mine Heart" (type this again). Time before
of apricots—i have love for each one reared.
not your only odds: baroque entablature
kissed on the ear, transported, spent
having no will to speak after put-down
flip disputing facts involving the other vowels
first showed alarm during carousel . . .
boil has burst end, fruit raised to take in taste
awkward—me too—as you feel it in your bones.

THE MESS

the mess i hate the most is the mess
i make myself i say to you
curled and farting. dawn's
early light means butting cathead,
purring humidifier, a kind of breeze—
and unconscious clenching.
back's wisp line clung to, kissed
blades cuz smooth—and the
fit! breasts interrupt but knees
fold into backs of knees
and buttocks connect
to back of stomach.
analogy is womb but drier.
we do too much, get worn
out so there's a kind of
jaggedness as crescents
under eyes . . . no leaves
on trees but buds that
make us plead oh trees
please please give us
your leaves i clean
the house. in the freest
possible mood i clean
the house. there is growling,
gaiety, disorder, ornament,
and any extra space we fill
with words. i can wash

the words off the fridge
but don't as there's a lot
of babaganoush and day
newly sunny we're both
at work. our children tear
the order into little pieces.
they are more parrots.
dailiness forks itself over
into the writing, trying
hard mannered but there's
a list of chores still undone
in the canter of the
universe. i see three
poles of how to write:
one stark, historical
one airy, fluid, with
lingerie, and then this,
the mugwump
who never stops writing
about writing cuz all
text is hypertext and i
have phenomenology
as eye is mouse when
attention as rollover
forces blossoms.
i want you to see this
as a kind of photoshop
document, with layers
i poke in the eye to
hide or reveal.

sucked along by
        f train into light
            mass buildings
                and parties, readings
the various empire lights
the young poets
now the sick old man
the jews the blue hat
the ponytail . . .
                "the white knucklebones
            assert themselves through
        skin" wrote my teacher's
sister. is that an angora
                    of rage? in what gear
                        can you go constantly
                            uphill? i notice i've
            grasped sisyphus's dick
            or why was he naked
            and straining (shining).
                sisyphus. are you
        corporate dragon lady?
or telecommuter?
            there are no longer any free
                boxes or communes although
        headscarfs are institutionalized
    as are foods in bulk or any other
                    calligram (mind, thought, will,
                attention, concentration) that pokes
        me in the arm. the computer
            engulfs me in cat litter

and cleanser, soapsuds, theory and
            dustmops. rags. i think of joan
                retallack, kathleen fraser, labor
                relations, my childhood in velvet.
the louder punk music when i'm
                near you sisyphus. i can smell
    the lunchmeat in your musky
        groin. sisyphus i smear you with
    avocado, with mayonnaise in lieu
        of subtlety, jerk you off with yogurt
and/or honey mustard. it is my task
                and i'm sorry i just can't write more
    carefully because i don't have any TIME.
    i'm standing in the second avenue station
now. now i'm on the train home. you are
    a beatle. you have the optometrist's gold
purse.   i don't need comic books;
    i'm an artist,
    surrounded by
                        psychos
        who are voyeurs in petal
garments, the petals
            fly off their sleeves to make
the carpet we
        walk upon the hangdog chaos
i pin my lower
                    lip upon and
hang there

                        suspended,

a pig artery
transplanted on my cheek, my tiny nipple
stretched waaaaaaaaaaaaaay out and

    looped around
    a grotesque

        painting of a pen
            i still somehow
            manage
            to write
            with.

BLAZE OF GLORY, SID!

you just don't love me
like you used to play the part
of the pearl diver on airs
in the bar i thought was
called "sociology." syntax
embeds itself with such
painful adjectives
in the end times. which
frees me to eat this particular
language and if i am petite
enough to argue with the
non-existent sacred texts
my eyeball will roam in
time to the slow rhythm
of animal tongues on human
fur the imbeciles love to
listen to. my beloved is
the discombobulated absent
sleepy animated seahorse,
i guess, anyway he's not here
and i don't know any mendel-
ssohn. give up enough to come
on to your friends as ruinous
surprise out of your own sneaky
interiority: décolletage, drool,

and the porpoises. maybe
i'm just cinnabar doormat
and he's the jade beercan.
juggling chakras way past
midnight mind all lit up
and warm with sound.
will he ever come home
to the revolving wooden
bird? fear sits big on the
eardrum of eurydice—
believe me. there's a whole
philosophy of salty secret
movement but to study
arcana just takes too much
time: matzoh bulls, shadow
puppies, linked vermin,
loggerhead sharks at peace:
city items morning breasts
out is it cynical enough
my verse again absolutely
flumpf flumpf: the devil
dislocate. the idea is to keep
the dolor moving and write
a very sunny verse. are you
tired of me now? give me
a raincheck and rain money
for my rainchildren. the shadow

of the falling man is luckier.
i am a falling blowing fennel
flower still with some flavor.
not big leaves of fouler cow
parsnip. i think
"o-shibori" and where
is my man. in a blaze. ghee
on the sensual surface of
things (curry). wily-ness.
shame. about love and conceit.
fractions. emotion as ghee/
greasing experience. topography
of licking the animal fur with
a human tongue: zoophilia
on the train to fire island and
a lynx lying on a plank. angry
about the social pin on the
background of acrid sleaze—
wormy garbage headache
elves, cheap trix of com-
bination—the sloppy overflowing
social craving and withdrawal,
niceties caked with maple.
there is no religion, nor self-
governance. i was more stoic
(exotic) as a consumptive
contaminant. the hot wind
came in from the hot plains.

it rained fire all week. the man
snores out drool. i need more love
but feel like a manic raging icicle
ricocheting off the walls of the dingy
domestic space. the energy is
dissipated at the taverns. the planet
venus is spat farther out by the sun.
she feels wrathful. she kicks. unfair?
is this literal, metaphorical,
allegorical, or totalizing? where is
the sun in the discourse? drunk
and snoring, ignoring the light
she uses to write:

speak to me in the language of
the sun, which is snores, galanga,
lemongrass. i won't listen to
anything else in my sprouting
anger that is a bag of small clams
in a net. label
stapled tightly shut
like a nut.

        only emotion infuses
        the room with that weird smell

        only emotion defers to itself

        only emotion endures the little grey
        falling-off points

internal scoreboard covered
with snakes: it's OK to be doing this
as wrong as this but you will need
to invent a convincing-enough
theoretical framework.

    i don't know. i feel young, no, old
    among paisley embryos. plus the blanket
    looks like warm cheese (+ rind)
    and i haven't any
    character(s).

hungry in the spongiform
rock i can't seduce the marvelous
(into the rigidity) (dignity)

my body's walls i forget
to be cosmic in wee hours
(fuck) the petrified tree, warm
chance, warm chalice, warm choice

      rhythm of snores
      on the hot flanks
      of old ermine

      passivity growling
      at odds

BLISSANDO

the city fakes itself
in mincing—i do too
much as croissant or
beagle—hey nouns!
inner tension makes
a noise i want to
harmonize to and
something roils,
but it's ok.
dancer moving in jerks,
not pretty but aggressive,
grinning. do you want to eat
the food in the pepper today?
that bleeds? or what. i have
a luck in kinds—aspirin
for kindred carrion . . . but
not "knocking." death smiles
at us from the studio.

starlight and smart
as gelatin, my
insolence is karma.
poetry rules the waves
the prison matron

paces—i know it
is artifice, but this
is a bit too much:
paste jewels
at Takashimaya . . .

the poem itself tries
to articulate a poetics
of the the the electronic
bird noises at the broadway-
nassau station (people
shoving by. in coats.).
standing is often a hardship
for people with dissonance.

smell of fast fried food:
matter becomes one
with other matter . . .
nothing but love
among the physics
against my particularly
pubic bone.

1) How is the vow
to be compared with the
hare as against such a pose?

2) The spiritually self-
protecting wonder pod.

3) Follow = God
Abandon = Gods

4) The anarchic snakes =
the scales of the asylum

noticing:
      men are plenty fluid too
      (urine spot,
      no undies)

DOMESTIC POEM

Gary draws Fanny Fandango
as the fan whirrs.
I'm in a black nylon slip.
ankles swollen up. I feel
a number of internal processes—
in heart, stomach, ankles,
& the forced clench of jaw
resting on my arm resting
on the bed as I write.
Don't you want to see
everyone have an orgasm
in the humidity? My head
jumps around. A little dome
on springs. A little dough
on a fingertip, and then,
sonic boom, poetry comes
out viscous, clear. I make
it make a string between
forefinger and thumb/
gee you're dumb.
The violets clamor
around angrily: now
is the time to reproduce.
Now is the time for
invasion of privacy.

Then the scales tip, and
whoa—! I steady myself
with arm movements,
jerky backwards circles.
The blush of sex is on
the babies, whose
personal frogs sit by
them watchfully.
I like layerings done
by means of prepositional
phrases: "on the babies"
"with arm movements"
"on springs" "between
thumb and forefinger"
"of prepositional phrases."
Gary jingles something
in the other room. I'm
drowsy, thinking
to combine DAISIES
and COMPASSION.
Now he's drawing
Lady Languish (language).
"It's too hot," he says,
"for oral sex."
It's too hot for the Age of
Enlightenment. Is it too hot
for Astroboy? Kierkegaard?

For the slow kind of thinking.
Now the (monsieur) testes
dangle down loosely, like
goobers in rosy, hairy silk.
The pink inside of a lip's
slightly blue blood bumps
and rattly music—HEY
TURN THAT OFF I can't
hear my poem. A series
of raspberries. Nemo
jumps up with a squeal,
OK, he can be in my poem.
Worrying an ingrown
hair on back of thigh,
its raiséd bump, and
spininess distributed
over butterflesh, the map
of what I contains, unfolds,
feeling my large intensity
pulse against the bed. Muscles
string through the harp(y) in
black nylon slip. All around
the air conditioners drip and
drone.

LORD DASHAWAY.

26 Why is an unbound book like a
     young maiden in bed?

HER PRE-HARP SHAPE IV

"What is identity if not the integrity
   of hollyhocks and separateness,
      whatever might be held inside
         the moat that divides one soul's
            territory from the Whippoorwills
            of other psyches?"

"Hey all! What's up! Under the fun
and been great!"

"Huh?"

                              "It's fatal liberality"

                "Telepathy"

"rhetoric"

                              "Made a growling sound"

"It was a piece of life, I said"

      "The man
      dancing
      ing her the
      features

smiling
obsequiously.
a flat
angry
look."

"Small World"

"So I'm from where"
    "Go around saying-smelling"
        "'That stinks!' more musically"
            "ointments"

"a soft curly beard.
You have grow a beard."

                "I'd heard and seen . . ."

"I want to laugh out loud,
HA! ha! just like that"

    "Yes.
    You are strange with it."

    "All this matters."

'SUBJECTIVITY'

i have interrogated
the lyrical subject
and found her winsome,
prone to seizures
when balancing
on the blasphemous tripwire
of her own sober critique . . .
but the podium she
crawls toward obscures
the genitals in the non-
maudlin* internecine
epephebian mist.
her chirping box
wants more conscience
but escapist from essence—
hey marxists, hey! truth +
beauty = the feel
of the city, described,
and all the people
sitting around vivid
talking warm as
creepy death in
potentia (but it's OK).

(*non-mammalian)

the possible lips
of social anxiety
not as symptom
but as utopian gesture
when you stand back
to view the endless
nested vestibule
of distances
through paper flaps—

as i don't need
satire at the moment
until the real revolution,
just clothes, servants,
horses . . . and light
humming . . . no . . .
what i need's a hasbro
munchkin feast,
a non-explicit sexuality
the thieves won't lunge at.
but i also exploit the urge
to lunge out of dissolute
resignation writ large
in my guilty character.

no animal in truck
that doesn't organize in
digestion—for more
stomachs, the curd
and rumbling dissent:

Dissent (ary)
Dissent [can] (ary) [an] (droid)
[diode] (rant) [her] (oin) [e] (tment)

∞

the shaggy horsefly
mounts the dissent
more conservatively—
loosened from my braid
lacking big black trunk
of sensuality cuz
restless:
the golden retriever
on expandable leash
thinks it's free.

two clones of toulouse-lautrec
walk across to the baseball diamond:
actually they're hasids.

        notion
        act
        speech
        tirade
        yelling

cathode
ray
excite
actual
marble

"the nipple-aureolar complex
is then positioned
to a higher level"

'INTERIORITY'

interiority's a raised surface—
edible, peeling . . . i shit . . .
gold . . . bumbling . . . people's feeling for
pineapple doesn't diminish
indignation/can't keep in regulation hat
or leave culture to fester (feather)
or slay dragons

when i look for the job
of sighs in urban flush—the people
and their pennies (penises) and waving

i make enough money to flirt
with aerial feeling 'tho i hear
a gradient spectrum and swabs of
arrangement:
the youth is not roiling and
rigidity is not a banner.

> faeries line the hallway,
> their pincers nimble.
> and faces sweet too.
> they make kisses at us.
> the night clacks.

events muscular and derivative—
in the double (doubted) world
of victims (urchins)

a word inserts itself
into my hands, fuzzy,
squirming, and the
never-closing yellow eye
of satire . . . beeps

candles assemble
in a circle . . . i straighten
my head,

i forget the blue spires
of description (occasion)
and the pancake hut

i can only follow it
(the curve) over agony
to cleanliness—the distance
measured in heaves

cool trance melting the
twilight i fart in,
a little sardonically

THE SCOOP

what do you make
of this? huge variation
in everything—i see
i accept their word
as legitimate yellow
bird with crest on
thick legs or red space
creature with circle
above head—cute—
intent look—everyone's
obedient—how come?

suddenly noticing
i'm made in china . . .
walking a line
of plastic wrap
between the twin
towers . . . actually
wanting . . . to be naked
with the grackles
and the noises they make
in my nightmare—
not horrific
but dull the baby
works its jaw as instinct

soon to be shopping
its way out of this
sandtrap, and i wish
it well.

i saw:

1) the glum faces of the couple
   in the morning—her backpack
   said "memories"

        and

2) the bottom fall out of
   "emotion as category"

we go on.

i don't know why
i am always wanting you—
someone—to have my interiority—
despite the vividly glowing taboo
burning the fabric of summer

with a master's ∞ degree
in admiration,   the sun shines
on the belligerent troubadors—
that's their reality—
opalescent green bowling ball
an unlikely argument
against psychotropes.

the three chambers
of the corruptible heart
flood with seriousness.
the onion's rotted
with psychology.
may you never frown
as you sleep:
intent of speaking pudding.

fireflies coiled mentally ill
guild dub thigu:

you want (i want) your mind
to wander into the white loaf (catamaran)

tales of the minx—
Decorate My Ass
with your policies.

CUCKOO-BRAIN

in sweet silent meadows
of foolscap, sun shines
rigorously: multiple choices
reveal your personality
to the multitudes, finally
brimming with that GOOD
irony everyone's on about—
the jack or lever.
i am really wrestling—naked—
with those institutions—
mmm hmmm—on the bright
sunny abusive day.

1) droner
2) everything they taught you was false
     was true

of the versifying urge:

an incessantly moving spider monkey
bares her teeth.

3) recuarge
4) loop-dee-loo

"i find this all terribly tiresome"
"shouldn't you be less eschatological"

fear of debate, hard balls, breakup
of matter into drab monads:

to fall back—not on god—
gatorade goes into body

i suppose the robot
doesn't want to walk

bagel . . .
goes into body . . .
people laugh . . .
at me . . .

people get sucked
through the hole
punched in time

people tilt . . .
their heads . . .

In All That Is ME,
  There Is a Seed of
MYSTERY.

  Virginia Slims
  Find Your Voice

real radicals
in the land of brands
full-throated celebration of
"pre-cognition"—this wondrous
"connexity"

markets boil down
to spectacle of authorized
dissidence—a crimson comet
i can listen to
while i drive

and so,
think different—
chickens in a man's trousers
tread luxuriously
on this bricolage . . .

the materials at hand
are combined karmic energies
of slippage, a litany of logos—
rude noises
in the museum of me

"are there gates around the city?"
"what if?"
"the foetus is undifferentiated"
"mode, meter, timbre and the like"
" i consider anarchism
   the most practical
   and beautiful philosophy"

8

you too can change
your silhouette—mine's
ragged, thoughtful.

to spontaneously
generate—do i need it?—
a reason for lilting

"halflife interdependent
prestidigitator," i say
to the starburst background

even the marchioness
eats. eating so primary—
kwashiorkor . . .

blue agave nectar—
i can't explain
the (chains of love) mechanism

or the borderless tone of lament
ringing through all classes—
like i can hear it . . .

i pretend to know
the hand may
go somewhere new

what about now?
humidity, salted fish,
dull expectation

and the missing limbs
of inspiration
found in artificial color

up will as is lush (light)
corruption are rife (light):
inflammatory. virgin. tangled. cup.

DICKY DAGGERWOOD.

1. Why is a melancholy young lady the
pleasantest of all companions?

HER PRE-HARP SHAPE V

If not an elephant's trumpet, my mind
might transmute the midnight roar into
leopards through the bars, to lick
and toy with—her back arched,
smelling of alcohol, byzantine,
instead of inside our rattling.

The marginal is often what's valued
later: exile's air of wistful, agile
dexterity. Aerialists did headstands,
chanting slave songs to keep their swings
falling in perfect tandem.

The shrimp-pink dawn was ours.

Trumpeting.

CAPRICORNUS

consciousness at angles
to itself—from the drug—
ungainly—scratched
feeling—cold guano
as visceral paste

scratched down the center
of the notebook's hot light
of composition

aware: of scampering, the
pink part darting but—
grooming—my pores—
stand on end in—
bardic—stutter—
puked—diamond—
on edible string:

small plastic crabs
a joy forever—
no horror to confess
today

everyone wants fireworks in their glibber hands
today, but my nausea's a distraction tactic from
the string of carefully worried nonchalant
abstract urban nouns.

tips of fingers just barely touch water's surface and
moving release shimmers sparks of light the pharaoh
prattles in the night.

i will not hold back
but spread my lips
on mossy rock
to suck the dew
that gathers there

dew—toes—grass—squish—
nature's rocky.

♑

pushing past the adolescents
in the doorway, their speckled . . .
analogies . . . the crowd of carrion
lotuses. sipping from an
asphodel as if bewildered,
all lights on me
in kingdom come.

"it's just not right"—
inevitability, that is—
or the string of effects
stolen from all genres:

G + RAM + MAR

can't the lines come faster?
isn't inspiration a greasy reed?
will i have taken off my clothes?

is . . .

       i want . . .

              rigatoni . . .

♑

i'll take irrelevance . . . over
the union of wholes.
i don't exactly know what
to think anymore about
nostalgia . . . for exoticism . . .
how futile the fight in
the mist . . . the . . . unremarkable
. . . delicto . . . of a series of
stills.

and if i am late for the ball again—
don't slurp that—or chew ice—
it's only with the weary irritation
of domestic slavery that anyone
"freshens up" anymore. and the
temptation to be "patently
unfriendly," to "waste words"—
to just sort of flop around in a
swarming nest of indicators . . .

not "more angry about money
than speed" but yes, PHYSICALLY
angrrrrry the bleach.

shiny taupe layers of pigeon sound
scratches stomach curly barbed wire
aquamarine tags, and more peeling.
scoop up language as raw thing—

i hate this . . . silvery
gunk . . . look of dolor.

he said, "the poem has a center" . . .
i feel sick . . . with chili oil? cigarettes?
pollen?
                    nape's curl . . . oh . . .

sufrir de una bad aesthetic. . .

        it's not the marvel of linked space
        in clouds and the bodily rivers
        in them, nor the actual claret
        of perfect runcibles . . . folded . . .
        under usual egret wings . . .

an agate also . . . forces my eye:

that puts me in this
               lactic mood

        when i think of you,
               my hips widen

into a soundbreak

i'm juggling a bomb—
with answers:

        yes, no, as if,
        don't ask, calyx

OSTRANENIE

(10/31/99)

(humming/ ocean bird noises/ ocean noises)

hakike no umi / sea of nausea

tetsugaku no umi/ sea of philosophy

nekojita no umi/ sea of cats' tongues

sozou no nai umi/ sea-with-no-imagination

poruno no umi/ sea of pornography

chikara no umi/ sea of power

nisemono no umi/ sea of artificiality

hiniku no umi/ sea of irony

kangae no umi/ sea of ideas

suimin no umi/ sea of sleep

namae no umi/ sea of names

tide is labor,
the drag of the dead star.
compulsion.
the water breaks,
creatures spill out.

heaves in limulus/ heaves out nudibranchia
heaves in ophiodea/ heaves out periphylla
heaves in gorgonia/ heaves out campanulina
craving noisome epibulia in toto

(TOTO + cackling)

the tide rises to the occasion, which is the beginning.
it is ghastly. ovary simple.
the cells are scooped out to give to the humans. each cell
gasps for the water it was wrenched from, looks at its human
with hollow eyes, tongue shriveled into a point.

(panting)

Horror = limitlessness
Limitlessness = utter objectivity

what can we learn from this?

a giant sea urchin gloms onto the polar cap, melting it—
expanding me

an intracranial silver fish is ostracized by the other silver fish to which
it is identical. this is an allegory about freezing black water, treasure
chests, ornamentation, goblets, bullion, the cauldron, the pearls that
were his eyes as magnets sticking the water to the earth etcetera, etcet-
era. this is not an allegory about me. although i am the ocean i enjoy
allegory because it is limited. every item has its corollary: VIRTUE
can be made to equal STROBALIA, and AULOGRAPHIS,
INCESSANT GNAWING.

a small grayish eel wiggles up from the brain coral and turns its head
to the left in order to look directly at you. it moves its body slightly.
the eel wants to lie flat across your shoulders, or coil at your thymus.

you are now at the borrom of the ocean.

elegance = depth (the cowering)

spiderlike, the thromboid hellion ouijas pathetically in
atonal sub-darkness

(noises)

the familiars curl the white-hot screws into living meat (hiss)

they have braided the earthworms
and are licking
their rosy gray membranes
into clumps of radioactive silt—

the finely ground poisons of
eyeless generations of
incessant commentators

with cat's head and crab's body
beelzebub scuttles past as a giant lesion
ringed by tiny glowing warts
on the forehead of a zombie axolotl
in an intellective orgy of one

and on whose nubile carcass
rivulets of discharge co-mingle with
vituperative oyster-colored spit
in cantilevered disinterested nibbling
at long intestines

exploding tubal preganancies hurl blood clots
onto the costly chandelier as asparagus
penii of maleficent leprechauns
burrow into the magma

pendunculated, the fibroid ego
twists on its stem
causing severe abdominal pain
and other dislocations

heads turn around and around and around
spewing glossolalia:

(allondiuneffrreennoosopapapipipolundifrrrrrgzzzzharaha)

the ocean disguises itself as a jew. a jew disguises herself as a piece
of bamboo with a hole in it. your mother is disguised as a raw
chicken wing. all other women are disguised as limp oily armfuls
of kelp. computers disguise themselves as pagan fancies, but insert
themselves into your personal circuitry and find ways to implode.
a turkey is disguised as a venusian. menace is disguised as pleasure,
and pleasure as menace. a shopping bag full of lotus roots, long
purple eggplants, and baby bok choy is a thin disguise for incendi-
ary yearnings. disfigured stalkers are disguised as accordionists.
protoplasm is disguised as the orange fluid that oozes from the
brains of dying marionettes. no disguise is as ruthless as the one
that covers the surface of things.

in the middle of things is a cold room. it is your worst fear.

a lurker with a heart like the suppurating anus of caligula fiddles
with a jar that can't be opened. the jar contains a living arrogance,
mouth open in a scream that seeps through the pores of the glass.
the arrogance has its little hands pressed against the glass, futilely
pounding, but everyone's ignoring it.

the lurker is obese with weasels that bite his scalp and hang there
in lieu of hair. blood streams down his pneumatic face over his
inverted u-shaped glistening watermelon mouth,
tongue pressed against fangs in effort.

the room is a locked refrigeration unit. goldfish periodically rain
down from the ceiling, sliming along the skins of the naked
orphans with no critical vocabulary.

some (goldfish and orphans) are living, albeit in epileptic
fluorescent squalor, and some are dead. d e a d .
the orphans that are alive sing a song like this:

> hebi no
> niwa ni
> ningyo ga tobu
> taiyo wa
> kaki ka?
> ara ma. . . .

the dead goldfish and orphans raise their heads to look at the
audience, chanting

THE DEAD SHALL LIVE
   THE LIVING DIE
      AND MUSIC SHALL
              UNTUNE

        THE   SKY

MADAME MANDOLINE.

24 Why is a baker like a grave digger?

Her Pre-Harp Shape VI

or

Smell Meat

Contaminate broken seed box;
"Fairish, in part," it describes a pupil!

Badly rated art we move nowhere.
As to being edited, "cheap shot" is set in superiors.

Very small, but that thing is a fork!
God drops right out of a felt-tipped pen.

Cream soda—me adding bit from W.C. Fields.
She-cat eventually reveals she's from hell—

Sounds like I'm to go back to get more grass;
Sounds like the only kind of music.

Mental repunctuation of a clue is the key to its solution;
It could result in a lot more fluttering in an organ.

ZOEA

in the inner ear a spool recondite
the watchers toe a bit upon.
hulks of manhood blurt out
confessions of strandedness,
then choose to discover orange
sundresses in rag or bone.
older bottles as magnitude
older bells as authenticity.

i see i need a picture in my head
of dad and mom as lonely word.
astounds glass how. that's just my
issue, i take the kale nevermore:
wart of bliss, hebephrenia.

a limitless number of calico cats ...
take no action whatsoever.
i play with them in the void.

homophonia elites my silver bug
raised to the clouds as morph.
chant = bitter genesis with mine smell.

self-conscious? you know it.
every time the fig hits the ceiling.
like how as blobby knobs of speech,
below own whisper, fish
almost have . . . summer.

strategically, what ejaculates?
the roots hit the sky . . .
if you really loved lyricism, you'd . . .
but I guess I'm a bundle of needs too.
looking for a form today,
my writing subliminally tight
under the looseness today.
the number of words happily
available to the red hat hair of
brains. treat the bee as brother,
someday you'll be honey.

creative maudlin not kicking
in over lola montez or maria
montez/ my education feels bad
today. who's boethius, boehme,
and what is the traffic of my roasted
insouciance.

trumpets nurse the mood
i try to catch to lean back
against wall feeling hair
swing, the tow truck a poem
for the new girl and his
problems on the detoxifying
avenue. i spend my days in
songing in strange hat and
i want to fill my mind
with gum and gossip
in simples.

suffering from an ecstatic
disorder, the salad dressing smells
of eyeglasses and where's
the typical party. i also
don't like the way it tastes,
now, elevate:

words are still the subject as pills
of cuneiform ranting
skin a tight network of criscrossed canals
the dry panting
my is a o no pass over seraph
of no confuse

did you change your noose
to swallow my devotee
is the best frock balance
a hero lapping a break?
heaven's insane recalcifying
by some soppy tone
yes i'm a bleed listen
you age sephardic country
humanities and how i louse —
oh you're kidding—
as no one else and how long
the window dove don't
if i'm asleep just in time

O

this enters the sphere
of the aesthetic with a giant gong

abrogating dumb tongue in
stilton. spermy artlessness in
high hat over the far-flung
conclusion

handprint glittery cheese—
the fries are wiggling: gelly
roll. over magda and bertram
how they are olive (alive).
in multiple drafts and stretching—
the hammock of sung.

aporitic verbiage sparrow
squatting, professorial. violet
and frightened wave of gas,
the denture of wonder.
i thought hard parasol.
on the drugs of education
in lockstep pagina tion.
when a great poet dies,
the shrimp weep.

i thought hard at the
mall. sound. image.
saturation. emeritus
nowhere. tutelage
a crutch and leg hairy
under cast like bright
disease of mother tongue
above the drone of mucosal

whinny. the traitors and
their spotted wings, their
radar squares as caged as
peace. such moody things
as slake the compress
of techniques, their
complex simple forms
apostolic, diastolic.

remind me to ponder those
internal impulses we barely
notice, i always come away
with sympathetic skin
in the urban underground.
i felt swept and escorted
hands whitewashed lofty
like pleasure boats in sympathy
with enfolded pagan wealth

and powerful rigidity of
movement, um, excuse me —
i group buildings, suspicious
bovine teachers, this reversion
to time in dusty related objects
imperceptibly safe. in salmon wrap.

i saw a blonde with heaped-up
hair yelling "memsahib" at the
omens that show themselves
as recombination. undistinct
predatory mammoths in floral
print dresses . . . a porthole
is carved into a whine. lunacy
flatters itself in new starts and
pinchedness, wave of blind
castles move this way, that way . . .

hey catullus—the lightning will be
in your world as curvaceous
disjunction. look good in your
executioner hat, the information
you can smell in ocean frappé . . .

but i'm not meant to birth or
bend it qua telephone wire.
longletters from the lord of
selves—i see a telephone in
the old bathhouse. any problems
with police nudity? rude squeak:

sounds are loud. O. O. O.
the women hit my bread. who
will paint the town olive, cambric
cranberry or paste? be more specific
about the dove blue and "she has no
sensibility."

I WANT MY BARE BREASTPLATE
covered in sand. the noble unveiling
of pure vinyl (value). no fine mesh cover
heaving defensively. in the garden a rake
of worms, all dead. i see a flash of light.
transfigured as kindness and soup with
yuba, under torii of relative meaning.
denser than paranoia. more kuyashii
than sphinx.

macaronic verse falls out the eardrum.
mosaicked on. its awkwardness makes me
jump (up and down) in a sparrow's
frame of references. the old pigeon
is miserable. i feel pigeon.

feeling streaks into body as something
missing, becomes old habit faster than
the stepped-on rake hits your head,
reverses personality so that
interiority juts out soda spills
out of buildings. disorder. but not
"crude"

neotericism has been well-done.
something else ground, formed
into patties, and grilled as
fabulous changes (crescent
moon and star. whispered
confessions in impatient
old age as each word crawls
on the back of the next).

processed and pressed self-
referentiality in lieu of ample
smiling human flaw. i hate
the whole tendency, want
grass huts under moon in
temperate weather. imposters
gnaw the bones of ancestors.
and are filled with prose. sick
of palimpsests, forever trapped
in lyric . . . it doesn't really hurt
but it hurts my throat.

reason as onyx says
i wrote from inner need
in caftan, juices lushing
in shit and bills and walked
to my mug, justice assigns

curfews to my children's
big broken light. the clouds
poked out at angles in
seraglio or put the pears
in sideways. i see a seabream
breathe out light. flies.
shakiness and pathos. in
a golden shift at midday,
transrational loose pigeons
dropt in soil. no draw lotus
here under sleep end. as
deepening or crescendo
nearly unzips skulls
so horns come greenly
out.

VALUE = AGE x RAGE

the id (blackened, many-limbed)
cartwheels in the pudding

the pomeranian yaps

eggheads line up
against the wall:

!!BOOM!!   *SPLAT*

the last Romantic totals them
with her plume:

"this enters the realm
of the aesthetic
with a giant gong."

"value is what can be eaten"

~

i have to pee

~

got that off my chest

they are reading (in
russian, chinese, or
history of zulu nation)

one chews a stick
of red licorice as
her eyes bore into

pages revered,
gingerly touched
by how their souls
get sucked

rimbaud
touches the cyclone
with windy docility

the voices in her head
as charcoal and
history (exhausted)

they don't stop yammering
the mighty sickle
they don't stop to yammer

permissive as b(r)easts
of the easts, who make
rhetorical figures in the air

over the head of
a sun-spun phantom
sidewinder blintz.

if i can say whatever
i want, the quick light
of intelligence furthers.

it's a little
reliable. a little
metaphorical "Q"

holding the opera
glasses. in my dry
mouth. hurtle through

feeling weird. where emotion
lies in the french clitoris.
think: garden salad, arugula . . .

queens and their minions
in a bar brawl with reason.
accompanied by orthodox zither.

i am thinking: biplane.
can you feel it? born again
as "flutter-dipping". cherry coke

as bombshell. anything
is anything else. anything
is anything. striation rides

its vessel in the skies.
it's "education"—the monsters
that the masks decide to wear.

i don't get anything cosmopolitan
out of hiding. the mud custard
and frantic—just released

trail of gems from asterisk
orifice. odd twitch in left hand.
tourette's baubles here in sync with

oooh . . . inflammatory . . .
loosening . . . of forehead
over ashes. scary man

on train in filthy red
sweatpants with boner—
brown paper alcohol and what

else to notice. how
the letter i edits my
plaything, and thoughts of space—

the sickness in it, a body
addicted to its gravity.

~

someone—get that brat
out of the panopticon!
i can't see the fighting

a small redhead at fisticuffs
with a beard—
in nowheresville, man . . .

the smoke of distance, anti-
gravity sickness. how do you
make a poem? or take a pill.

here's the part about the genitals—
well-thumbed. the first thought
snarls at the next thought,

and the cuckoo in the nest . . .
swallows everything. Eyes enlarge
in eternity. The future is bright.

✡

WHY NOT MAJOR BIRDS

prospect park
starlings doing catcalls.

i give a man a dollar
he says he'll use for chicken
soup

"i bring chaos wherever
i go (longing for hyper-
organization)"

i write to form
a community inside me—
of weirdos and their targets.
they are linked as cutouts,
i won't say membrane, but . . .
squid.

?

i was thinking of writing poems
as the process of foiling thought,
that is, following anti-thought

the thought stops, i foil it.
no it doesn't stop it rushes by
i've stepped out of the way

to show how i hate the powers
that bee.

?

writing contains anarchy,
breathes it out. i used to think
"i bring chaos wherever i go"
was a bad thing.

i'm sorry
about the neurosis part.
you'll just have
to get used to it.

jealous of their
objectivities.

the neurosis
is a gloved hand that reaches up
to cover my face.

?

there's something strange
inside me, a shadow figure
with a wisp for a body,
a brushstroke body, and face
a hypnotic spiral.

and feeling far apart from space.

i quickly lose interest
in my pubic hair
which hurts.

come on and lose
your little head
i want to join the discussion.

O

everyone wants inclusion
in the mute dialogue.
so they stand in a circle
at the party shuffling their feet.

i find i am attracted to the WORMATIVE
and CURSIVE FAITH curtain
of lies we wear over our private parts.

eeep—antlers,
and the language as material
falters the barest premise.

it's a monolith again
on my loose skin

so i write a sidelong smile (simile) in,
of phosphorus and tickling

~

nemo steps on my hair
i'm tired i'm not tired.

there is a sound restless in the bed
making sound.

faint jingle of
in the "tidepools"

you lost me there . . .

eucalyptus

p.s. i like the effect
of the tail

d
r
i
p
p
i
n
g

d
o
w
n

i
n

a
r
t
i
c
u
l
a
t
e
n
e
s
s

Born on January 14, 1964 in Oakland, Nada Gordon spent a semi-nomadic childhood in Northern California. In 1988, she moved to Tokyo, and returned to the USA in 1999. She is the author of More Hungry (Voces Puerulae, 1985), Rodomontade (e.g.,1985), Lip (Voces Puerulae, 1988), Koi Maneuver (1990), Anime (Voces Puerulae, 2000), Foriegnn Bodie (Detour, 2001), and Swoon (with Gary Sullivan, Granary Press, 2001). She lives in Brooklyn with Gary Sullivan. Samples of Nada's work appear on her website at www.jps.net/nada/nadaroom.